T0194029

FOR THE
Broken Heart

JESSICA MARKIEWICZ

authorHOUSE®

AuthorHouse™
1663 Liberty Drive
Bloomington, IN 47403
www.authorhouse.com
Phone: 1 (800) 839-8640

Published by AuthorHouse 07/07/2020

ISBN: 978-1-7283-6591-6 (sc)
ISBN: 978-1-7283-6590-9 (e)

My Last Walk

The last walk
Down memory lane
Trying to find questions
Catching myself crying and alone
From the good and bad times
Built over the years together
Leaving everything behind us
With nothing but memories
Created together as a couple

Leave you Behind

Leaving you behind
For a new life change
Nothing left behind
But the shedding of tears
From the anger and emotions
Created from a life change
Without anyone's comforting love
For the exception of God's love
Through life obstacles

The Unanswered

I sit here alone
Wondering what I've done wrong
To ruin a happy life
With the man I thought I knew

Why did it come to this?
I became a wife for a reason
To start life with a man I loved
And build memories through the years

I have no answers
To questions being asked
As I look upon myself
To become a stronger woman

But I will promise myself
To continue my faith in God
Through life obstacles given
To strengthen myself within

Life Obstacles

Waiting in a quiet room
Fear of anger and anxiety
As my body becomes nervous and numb
Wondering if he will return
As he has broken my heart
To begin life obstacles
Questioning about my future
And if I will ever
Have a second chance
To be happy again and loved
For whom I become of
As my eyes fill up with tears
With questions unanswered
For the one and only exception
Having faith and confidence in God
To walk me through this
During my life obstacles

The Love of my Life

I married a man too early in life
And wasn't prepared for the responsibilities
I thought he loved me, and we would be fine
As we married young and our love would grow
When we would begin creating life memories

A couple years begin to pass as things were fine
When a time came that would take away my smile
And he went out and cheated on me, and I deserved more
But with a heavy heart, and at a young age
I decided to take him back despite his cheating

We struggled through the years together
As my heart was still broken from first time
I struggled to find trust through the lies
But driven by fear, I mistakenly thought
Things would change for the better

Now that I'm on my own in life
I look back to be grateful for many things
That we had no children together or major assets
I begin to examine my life in many different ways
For my relationship has failed, for that I am sad
But the result of this could never be bad

Future Love

Often times I sit and wonder
If love would ever find me again
For my heart has been ripped
Into a million pieces
As it seems no one cares

Trying to understand the pain
That couldn't be explained
Through the tears
Beginning to drip down my face
As the truth is exposed

Finding someone who cares
Will take time for me
As I continue to ground myself
And find my place in life to love
Again, during this time of healing

He's All Yours

He tells you his secrets
You will want to believe
He will tell you all his lies
That you will never know it was a lie
When you talk to him on the phone
And begins to hypnotize you to believe

He was a married man
With a wife and no children
Tried hard for a child of our own
As we were unable to accomplish
Through our years together
Through thick and thin

He left me and our marriage
Because he felt you were better for him
As he begins to encourage you
To fall into his lies he shares

Why would you want him
Who wants you to believe his lies
That begin to seek behind the truth
Wouldn't you want a man to trust
Whom has become very sneaky
And hides a lot from his loved ones

Take precautions when talking to him
As you don't know the truths
And probably never will
As he claims he is innocent
And has done nothing to hurt me
Through the years we spent together

You should know better
Than to encourage men for attention
As they will believe everything
When we had our shares of problems
But you have hypnotized his mind
To see the ugly and walk away

Making promises out of guilt
Then believe and trust him
For what you assume is the truth
He will have you hypnotized
Before you find the truths
Behind the man he truly is

So, no matter what happens
I will grow myself to be stronger
And sit back and begin to watch
As your fun with him lasts
When your relationship with him dies
Because now he's all yours!

Strangers

Death approached in our marriage
Ugly words were spoken
Creating pain and depression
As the holes on the heart
Are created from the news broken
Emotions beginning to shatter
As we begin to sweep them away
To ending our marriage
As our emotions are torn at this time
Let's walk by each other
And smile as we become strangers
During the time of healing our hearts
And beginning to move on with life

Hurts to Smile

I put a smile on my face
When heading outside
And my friend sees the pain
In the eyes full of tears
Trying to stay positive
As I become alone now
And try to act normal
As if nothing is wrong
Knowing you are now gone

Putting a strain on me
When I smile and it hurts
Thinking we were doing well
And now you tossed everything
From memories created over the years
To shattering everything, we had

I laid my eyes on you
And a loss of breath
When I fell in love with you
Then I lost my breath yet again
When you walked away
And hurts to breath
With the pain that won't go away
As I try to heal the damage

I don't see you coming
Back into my life as I wish not too
Done enough damage and hurts
When I look back at everything
Wondering what I did wrong
To deserve my heart to be shattered
Which will make me stronger person
Knowing it hurts when I smile

Broken Heart, Broken Dreams

Broken heart, broken dreams
Turning into silent screams
My heart begins to screech
Into broken pieces
How it begins to destroy
And everything begins to fall apart

If you begin to look back
Into my terry eyes
You will then realize
What you've done to hurt someone
To leave everything you had
To begin a new life elsewhere

I wanted to go back to the beginning
When we were first dating
And before my heart and dreams
Have been broken through a shock
That things would begin to take a toll
And my cries would not be heard

I begin to sit back and think
About the good memories created
As I try to heal the broken pieces
For I am lost without words

To begin finding happiness again
I never dreamed of this
To experience a broken heart
And goals that I dreamed about
I will begin to reach back in
To give the pieces of my heart and dreams
That has been destroyed

Memory Lane

As we sit here in silence
No longer as husband and wife
I can't forget that moment
You asked me to become your wife
And sit back and look at memories
That we created over the years together
Begin to fill my eyes of painful tears
Knowing my heart has been broken

We have spent so much time together
Looking upon our future as a family
And having children of our own
As we encouraged each other
Through our college years
I begin to look back at moments
When you didn't understand the terminology
As this was not your field of interest
You encouraged me to do better

As my heart has been broken
And you have left me for something better
I can't forget the happy times
That I spent with you over time
Whether it was good or bad
But ahead, the best it yet to come

As I held you in my arms
I never dreamed of letting you go

You may have broken my heart
But I will get back up and heal
Stronger than I ever been
As my future begins to call
Our memory lane beings to fall
With nothing left to say
Life together begins to end
When walking through memory lane
Reminds me of things we have done

The Unknown Questions

I know you have left me
For a new and better life
But you don't begin to see
How this breaks my heart
Since now that we're are divorced

My heart breaks in the dark
With questions unanswered
Waiting for my heart to heal
As we shared all these years
Begins to disappear as no one cares

We had a love so strong
People couldn't believe
As the news was broken
That we would get a divorce
After the years we spent together

I lie here and cry at night
With fear of anxiety and anger
Wishing I had a should
To lean on my side
To help me with healing of my pain

We begin to move on
With new life changes
As the broken pieces
In my heart begin to heal
For a chance in life
To become happy once again

Wishing it Away

I begin to wish it away
Hoping for a new life change
As I tried with no hope in sight
Feeling discouraged and lost
As I didn't want to lose
My only close friend whom I married
For the hope of a change in himself

I wanted change for the better
As I wished it away
From feeling down and depressed
And nowhere to go in life
When instead my wish
Would eventually be granted
And my life would change forever

No pill could erase
The pain my heart has felt
When I begin to look back
What I could have done differently
And to begin to say to myself
Be careful of what you wish for

You're not Alone Hunny

I went through the divorce
Never imagining the results
Through the struggles to come
With stress and emotions
When being told you're not alone

Always remember to never give up
Everyone goes through obstacles
And challenges thrown at us
Remember to think positive
Even through struggles in life changes
As you are never alone

He broke my heart when he left
Leaving behind the shattered pieces
Of my heart as it was my fault
And I would be alone
Fighting off the tears of sadness
And reminding myself
Others been through this and
You are not along hunny

Missing You

Walking up in the moment
Looking over to my side
To see the person, I wanted
Until I reach my disappointment
Seeing that you are nowhere

Beginning to realize the truths
That we have departure our ways
And I would begin to face reality
That I know you will never return

My heart has been torn
No one can replace
As I begin to recover
Without my love of my life

As we began to depart
And begin a new life
You took a piece of my heart
Leaving me behind with shock

I always thought
That you would never hurt
Me the way you did
As you left me behind

I begin to break down
Into many teary eyes
Struggling through each night
As I miss your comfort

We begin to build
A new life without
As I begin to learn
Who I am as a person

Our Time Has Come

Throughout our time together
I thought you were the one
To pick me off my feet
As we said our vows
To dedicate our lives together
As you said many lies
I still fought to stay strong
Through the ups and downs
We begin to face our challenges
As we are no longer
Able to fight to stay strong
And cause us to leave
Each other's heart for good
For someone whom we believe
Would be a better fit as
One would begin to suffer
From the emotions and anxiety
When asking many questions
To why this had to come
As we shattered our vows
And departed our ways

Looking Back

Looking into my eyes
What do you see?
Don't let the looks fool you
As you may not know
The pain you put me through
Fighting off this depression
As I fight back tears
When thinking about my past
And what I could've done differently

I was young when I married
I was swept off my feet
Walking down the isle
To say my vows and I do
In order to spend my life
With the one I loved

Throughout the years
We fought to stay strong
As you couldn't handle the stress
Beginning to trigger lies
Leading to cheating
That would begin to rip
My heart into bits of pieces
For myself to pick back up

You never see the struggles
That I went through
To keep our marriage strong
Before it would get shattered
And my life would turn around
To a new future of challenges
During my recovery stage
As I'm fighting back tears
Wishing this never happened
To a beautiful woman
Like myself and others

It's Okay Not To Be Okay

During a time like this
When struggling in life
During a major change
Beginning to remind yourself
That it is perfectly okay
Not to be okay
As we fight off emotions

This becomes a time in life
To begin reflecting ourselves
To inhale the future of things
And exhale our past regrets
As we begin to think positive
About the changes that would
Be for the souls of our hearts

It is also a good time
To exhale the past as
It begins to bring you down
From moving on with life
And facing new challenges

You Will Never See me Fall
You will never see me fail
Even though it may be hard

And I may struggle through it all,
You will see me come back stronger
As no man will take me down
Through emotional stress
As I learned to never give up
And continue to have my faith
Even though you may see me
Struggling to stay positive within
You will never see me fall
Into the lies of a man

Letting Go of the Painful Screams

Put your mind at ease
Breathe in the fresh air
Let the breeze blow
Through the roots of your hair
Let your eyes be opened
To all the futures beauty
Letting out those painful screams
Pounding within our hearts
Of the deepness of our souls

As you open your eyes
When you no longer feel the pain
Begin to breath in the fresh air
As the future begins
And let the darkness fade away
When you no longer
Feel the painful screams

I Am Who I Am

I am who I am
Because of what I have done
To achieve in my life
As I may be struggling
I am stronger than ever
I need nothing else
But my strength and soul
As no one will take me down
I would withstand them all
Through the darkest paths
I will walk over failures
Like those who never give up
To face life's challenges
As I become who I am

Divorce Me

You told me it was better this way
As we were better apart
To begin a brand new start

I need to let it out
As I wanted to begin to shout
It makes it better for everyone near

Asking many questions, wasting my time
Being told to say what's on my mind
As people begin to wonder, what has happened?

People told me to move on
As it didn't matter about my thoughts or needs
When I need help well indeed

As my heart begins to heal
People will understand how I feel
When our lives begin to departure

I Am Me

I am me
I am enough within
With no one's approval
Just me alone

I am strong
Through the darkness of light
I am boundless, and yet
Full of joy and delight

I am complete
No one holding me back
I am who I am today
Without anyone's consent
I am me.

Two Roads

Two roads were chosen
One was taken, one left behind
To be forgotten, long as I stood
Looking down one as far as I could
As my hopes would become frozen

No end to the light of the tunnel
As there would be no turning back
Walking through the dark path
As there's no end walking in the funnel
I begin to get lost and lose my track

Sorry I couldn't travel both paths
I stayed behind looking ahead
As there was no return turning back
And you begin to leave a footpath
For someone who is a hothead

Change

We all experience changes in our lives
Changes we look forward to and no one fears
No one can make those changes
But for yourself to make the decisions
As we make changes and begin to strive
As our time will come to an end

Change may depend on someone
As we begin to choose the path
To a negative or positive change
For us to make a better life
When it will affect us in the long run
Wash away negative changes in the bath

The Past

I remember the day we met
Too young to understand and see the danger
I didn't know the devil you would become
As you have filled me with so much anger

At first you gave me comfort within
To erase and numb me from the pain
As I thought I began to fall in love
Before the light you gave me began to fade away

You have hypnotized me into a trap
As I am not the only one to fall
So many friends made, forever gone now
When there is no one left to call

Dragged me to the rock bottom
As I lost my dependence on you
And there would no longer be a possibility
To solve and heal our problems

Every day I woken up to you
With only you on my mind
Desperate for your passionate love
Takes my breath away beyond and above

Through our times we spent together
I began to watch you steal my soul
As everyone began to warm me
When you began trying to destroy
My soul and heart as a whole

You left me broken and shattered
As my scars began to grew
From the emotions shattered mentally
While the number of wasted years flew

You erased and shred my future of hope
When everyone began to turn their backs
It was difficult to escape this dark hole and cope
As it is impossible to defend against your attacks

Reasons for the Past

The past is the past for a reason
Where it is supposed to stay
Some are unable to let go
In their heads it begins to eat away

Until all their focus becomes
The person they are comes clear
After their mistakes makes them fear
When there is no turning back

No matter how hard you try
No matter how hard you cry
And no matter how hard you think about it
You can never change the past

Don't let the negative wrap you up
What happens in the past
Happens for unknown reasons
During times we realized we screwed – up

The past is the past for a reason
So, don't hold grudges now that it's gone
And it is not time to pick up those pieces
Left in the past and begin to live on

People Cry

People cry when they are angry
People cry when their forgotten
People cry when they are depressed
I cried when you left my heart
For someone else better
Nothing could replace anything
For the love that we had
When it became neglected over time
Always remember this one thing
Better things are to come

Love Addiction

Together, we have done a lot
Until the moment we went through
When we couldn't take it anymore
As my heartbreak began to grow
And begin to look through the open doors

You came to me with promise and joy
When you picked me up from my feet
As my love for you was so strong
Now you take it and begin to destroy
When it was time for you to cheat

Why can't you just go hide
As I'm no longer your bride
And when I sit and wonder why
How you ripped me apart and landed me a hand
When everyone at home didn't understand

You promised me heaven and sent me to hell
When you ruined me and wished me well
Now I can go along on my way
I begin to break away painful chains
As I begin to wash away my pain

Remember

Remember the memories created
When we first became a couple
As a million tears began to fall
Thinking you were the one

Remember the things we've done
Encouraging each other through the years
When it created a lot of fear
Hoping for positivity to come in the long run

Remember what you have done
When you became the left wing
But never forget this one thing
Remember who was your loved one

I am Sorry

I am sorry for this has happened
As it hurts for me to heal
When it makes me sadden
That you are no longer there

You have not yet noticed how strong
You made me as an individual
That you are not alone
And you let the true you be shown

Your heart has been stained with dirt
Breaking my heart during your escape
When you saw that my heart has been hurt
As you tried fixing it with scotch tape

Coming To An End

I lye here awake tonight
Wishing things, I could change
As I become blinded by the day light
When it becomes so strange
For when life takes a change

Is it me, or is it you?
Do I try, or are we through
We shared a lot through the years
To leave behind and walk away
When it was best not to stay

Why we do this hurting the other one more
Only to watch one walk out the door
When you begin to play with my heart
Pushing each other to a breaking point
Leading us to separate apart

Is this the end or the beginning
When my head starts spinning
Only one could guide me
When I decided to flee
During my changes in life

This is what plays in my head
When I begin to wish it away
I look up into God and begin to pray
As I lay down and close my eyes
For its time to just go to bed

Don't Wait

Treat me with love and compassion
As I'm healthy vibrant and alive
Don't wait until its too late
To love me the way it's meant to be
See the beauty in my life and soul
When we begin to see each other as a whole
Don't begin to talk to me that way
As if you didn't want to stay
When I listened and gave you support
Take this and utilize our time
Before it becomes wasted years
Feeling like we just committed a crime
Now my heart has been broken
When the unknown words are spoken
To creating so much hate
As I begin to life off this weight

During My Time Away

During my time away
I cried every night
As a million tears fell
When my heart wasn't right

During my time away
It was time to heal
As there was nothing left to feel
When my heart has been broken

During my time away
I stepped foot on stage
As things went on
And life would turn a page

During my time away
It was hard to move on
Knowing it was killing me
Which would only make me strong

During my time away
A lot of things have changed
Causing me to rearrange
As I learn that I am alone

During my time away
I learned to be alone
And to stand on my own two feet
Wishing you'd sit in my seat

So now I spent time away
Realization would begin to display
At this stage in life
Still coping with strive

And on how I wish that
Things were different
That I could go back
To a time in the past
During my time away

Forget the Past and Start Fresh

I want to start fresh
Forgetting this pale and past
From the wicked world I lived in
Forget the past and start fresh

I want to erase and begin to forget
The memories that make me sad and weak
But learn how to use it as my strength
Forget the past and start fresh

Forget the mistakes and regrets
Not the lessons learned from them
When I cried silently, but not aloud
As I try to erase the storm cloud

Forget the past and start fresh
As this began to eat out my flesh
Find myself and begin to explore
As you emerge and shine like never before

Emotional Recovery

You have left me for someone else
Leaving me with questions unanswered
To have trust in someone I love
You began to see the person and was enamored
When my love began to get pushed and shoved
As if none of our love has happened

Tears begin welling into my eyes
As if there is no end
And my love for you dies
No one around to give you comfort
The hate you created, I badly despise
We are no longer the best of friends

Feel Lost

I began to feel lost
As everything was just tossed
When it seemed, nothing has happened
When I would become saddened

Entering the room into darkness
No one around to look at
As you would become so heartless
And that would be that

Beginning to look down the tunnel
As I would begin to chuckle
For the nonsense problems you built
Causing me to feel some type of guilt

When I begin to feel lost
Finding myself ways to get picked up
Continuing to keep my head up
During the times I feel like I been tossed

Shattered

It is lying all around me
Shattered into useless pieces of my heart
That could not rip my unprotected feet
It was the piece in which I lived for
During a fairytale story that would
Soon be shattered when difficult to understand
The realization it would become to be
As it would only become a fantasy dream
When I thought you truly loved me
For when my heart would feel the pain
From my own unspeakable distress
As you ram into my walls
With nothing left but to fall
Picking up the shattered pieces
You left from my broken heart
As it has now been shattered

I've been Around

I am the woman always too young to be
I packed my bags for coming and going
As if you have never cared
And going much further than ever before
I begin to find myself elsewhere
As this place is a problem
Filled with lies and unhappiness
Packing me with teary eyes
When the truth begins to prevail
And there will be no turning back
As my future a waits for a life change
When I continue to keep my feet going
And continue to face many life changes ahead

Over You

You were like a dream come true
That I wished I have slept through
I thought that you were a keeper
As I began to fall in deeper
Than to let go our love together

You say that you are over me
I now see you with someone new
When I though my dreams came true
Now its their chance to walk in my shoes
As for someday I'll be over you

What is Love?

Love has abandoned me
As I fall down to my knees
Left with questions unanswered
To why must I love him still
Still gives me the chills
When I realized it's he, I can't trust
To its time when I leave is a must
He is the one who chose to leave instead
Has love forgotten me?
When I gained my wings and became free
To give my life a brand new start
Finding someone else to steal my heart

My Heart

Perhaps I never loved enough
If only I loved much more
I would not nearly suffered as much
Left waiting, for you to change

If I only given my heart away
To someone who I would love
It would be safer left in parts
But now you have taken it all with you

Broken Wing

I have a broken wing
Damage done has been seen
I want to start new and feel new things
When you stop me to start a scene

Motivated to move, as I fear I'd fall
When I hide like there's nothing wrong
As I move, I begin to crawl
And I begin to sing my song

There a time for you to dry my tears
As you don't know what just happened
When no on left to help my fears
For something you couldn't imagined

Long Rainy Day

Long rainy June day
Watch the rain come down
From the cheeks of my face
As I begin to find my place
And then here I begin to pray
That the rain won't let me drown
When I enter a stage of depression
I begin turning my faith to God
As he has given his confession
People would begin to applaud
When there is no longer any pain
For the breaking for the chains
I sit down and begin to kneel
As he lets me begin to heal

That Young Lady

I was that young lady
You saw sitting on the steps
Looking out into the open world
With the long pretty summer dress
As my emotions would soon be expressed

I would begin to look at you as shady
As I wish not to walk in your footsteps
For the pain and feeling of being hurled
I would soon find myself blessed
When I no longer feel depressed

Losing You

I sit at the edge of the steps
With thoughts flowing through my head
As I begin to think positive
For changes that are to begin
During the time you begin to departure
For someone else you love
You begin to leave me behind
With nothing but wonders
When the tears begin to drop
And all I could think about
Is what I've done to lose you?
For a time for me to reflect
As I begin to heal the broken heart
You have left for me to cure

Let Begin to Breath

Begin to look at the skies
Release the negative from your spirit
When things seem to be hard
And the tears begin to fall
As your lungs fill with air

Let go of those watery eyes
When you begin to clear it
As you build up and guard
During the time to haul
And to find that prayer

Our eyes are full of joys and cries
When we learn not to fear it
And begin to flip over that card
When no tears are left at all
For the freshness that is so rare

Never Give Up

When things go wrong never give up
Even when things seem to go downhill
Stay strong holding the victory's cup
During the time of a standstill
As life gives its twists and turns
And we continue to learn and grow
During the time when the pace seems slow
For the time we deserve to earn

Often times we struggle and given up
When we feel we've been turned inside out
Always remember to reach for that smile
As it's not the end of the world
For a time for us to keep our heads – up
When you feel there is no more doubt
To reach for the skies and begin to fly

I Am Nobody, Who Are You?

I am nobody, who are you?
The way you hurt me the way you do
Leaving me behind with the painful screams
Ripping apart my beautiful dreams
Letting you tear me apart
After you realized you haven't gone far
As you would take me as a whole
And leave me with nothing but my soul
When I begin to grow and recover
For when my emotions will soon be discovered
With what you have out me through
As many people wondered and had no clue

Get Through It

When you're up against trouble
Feeling as you been displaced
Begin lifting your chin up high
As you begin to set your shoulders
Meeting the problems, face to face
To beginning to ask questions to why

Even when your future seems to grim
Never let your nerve deserve you
As the worst is bound to happen
Keep yourself in trim
As running from it won't save you
And remember to begin to strap – in

When you begin to see the sighting
Begin to let go of those emotions
Settling your mind and soul at ease
As the end comes from the fighting
When you no longer have his devotions
And your healing becomes a breeze

It All Went Down Hill

It began to go all down hill
As I stood at a stand still
Feeling the chains of locks
When I begin to hear a knock
With no one longer around me
And I begin to become free
For the time you put me through painful tears
During a time, I will no longer fear
When there is no longer jingling of the chains
And there no longer any strain
For they have become broken apart
To let the breeze come through
As a sign of relief and freedom
When the painful tears are no longer
A part of my broken heart

Printed in the United States
By Bookmasters